Sports Illustrated KIDS

STARS OF SPORTS

T0024113

KATIE LEDECKY

SWIMMING LEGEND

by Ryan G. Van Cleave

CAPSTONE PRESS
a capstone imprint

Published by Capstone Press, an imprint of Capstone
1710 Roe Crest Drive, North Mankato, Minnesota 56003
capstonepub.com

Library of Congress Cataloging-in-Publication Data
Names: Van Cleave, Ryan G., 1972- author.
Title: Katie Ledecky : swimming legend / by Ryan G. Van Cleave.
Description: North Mankato, MN : Capstone Press, [2025] | Series: Sports illustrated kids stars of sports | Includes
bibliographical references and index. | Audience: Ages 8-11 | Audience: Grades 4-6 | Summary: "At just 15 years old,
Katie Ledecky won her first gold Olympic medal. Since then, she has added nine more Olympic medals and 21 world
championships. She has also broken 16 world records and has the most individual world swimming titles of all
time-more than any man or woman in swimming history. Dive into this inspiring sports biography and learn
all about Katie Ledecky and her legacy"—Provided by publisher.
Identifiers: LCCN 2023054268 (print) | LCCN 2023054269 (ebook) | ISBN 9781669076513 (hardcover)
ISBN 9781669076612 (paperback) | ISBN 9781669076629 (pdf) | ISBN 9781669076643 (kindle edition) | ISBN
9781669076636 (epub) Subjects: LCSH: Ledecky, Katie, 1997—Juvenile literature. | Women swimmers—United States—
Biography—Juvenile literature. | Women Olympic athletes—United States—Biography—Juvenile literature. Classification:
LCC GV838.L43 V36 2025 (print) | LCC GV838.L43 (ebook) | DDC 797.2/1092 [B]—dc23/eng/20231130
LC record available at https://lccn.loc.gov/2023054268
LC ebook record available at https://lccn.loc.gov/2023054269

Editorial Credits
Editor: Christianne Jones; Designer: Jaime Willems; Media Researchers: Morgan Walters and Svetlana Zhurkin;
Production Specialist: Whitney Shaefer

Image Credits
Associated Press: Chris Carlson, 24, Lee Jin-man, 15, 19, Mo Khursheed Media, 10; Getty Images: Clive Rose, 5, Michael
Reaves, 23, Quinn Rooney, 28, The Washington Post/Toni L. Sandys, 7, 9, 11, 13, Tom Pennington, cover, Washington
Nationals/Patrick McDermott, 17; Newscom: Kyodo, 20, Sipa USA/Insidefoto, 27; Shutterstock: Kabardins photo, 25,
Snapper 68, 1; Sports Illustrated: Robert Beck, 16, Simon Bruty, 8

Source Notes
Page 8, "She is a fierce competitor . . . " "Training of Katie Ledecky, Swimming World Editorial Team," July 5, 2021, https://
www.swimmingworldmagazine.com/news/training-of-katie-ledecky-a-glance-at-workouts-that-led-to-first-olympic-title,
Accessed June 2023.

Page 16, "I had a lot of fun . . . " Karen Crouse, "Katie Ledecky Crosses into the World of Pro Sports. It Feels Like Home,"
New York Times, August 9, 2019, https://www.nytimes.com/2018/08/09/sports/katie-ledecky-swimming.html, Accessed
June 2023.

Page 18, "I was incredibly disappointed . . . " Inyoung Choi, "Katie Ledecky owns her time," *The Stanford Daily*,
May 4, 2020, https://stanforddaily.com/2020/05/04/katie-ledecky-owns-her-time, Accessed June 2023.

Page 26, "I'm lucky to have a family. . ." Inyoung Choi, "Katie Ledecky owns her time," *The Stanford Daily*, May 4, 2020,
https://stanforddaily.com/2020/05/04/katie-ledecky-owns-her-time, Accessed June 2023.

Page 28, "There's so much more . . . " Coy Wire and George Ramsay, "Katie Ledecky says she 'never would have imagined'
her Olympic swimming success," CNN, August 2, 2021, https://www.cnn.com/2021/08/02/sport/katie-ledecky-tokyo-
olympics-spt-intl/index.html, Accessed May 2023.

TABLE OF CONTENTS

Words in **BOLD** are in the glossary.

THE OLYMPIC UPSET

Swim fans packed the London Aquatics Center in England. It was August 3, 2012. Katie Ledecky of team USA warmed up near the starting block. She was just 15 years old. It was her first Olympic Games. She was about to swim in the women's 800-meter **freestyle** event. One of her opponents was the former champion, Rebecca Adlington. Everyone was sure Adlington would win.

Ledecky took a deep breath. The crowd's cheers filled the air. Ledecky knew her family and friends were watching. The whole world was watching.

"Take your mark!" said the announcer. *BEEP!*

Ledecky dove into the water. She swam like a champion, breaking away from her competitors and leaving them in her **wake**.

Sixteen laps later, Ledecky realized she'd almost broken the world record. When all the **heats** were done, Adlington ended up with a bronze medal. Ledecky won the gold. It was one of the biggest upsets of the London Olympic Games.

〉〉〉 Katie Ledecky reacts after winning her first Olympic gold medal.

FACT

Ledecky's winning time for the 800-meter freestyle was 8 minutes, 14.63 seconds. It was the second-fastest time in history.

CHAPTER ONE

YOUNGER YEARS

On March 17, 1997, Kathleen (Katie) Genevieve Ledecky was born in Washington, D.C. Her parents, Mary Gen and David, were always there to support her. Her mom had been an excellent swimmer in college. Swimming was in Ledecky's blood.

Ledecky's older brother, Michael, also loved swimming. They took their first swim lessons together at the Palisades Swim and Tennis Club. At age 6, Ledecky had a goal. She wanted to swim to the other side of the pool without having to stop. She kept trying until she could do it.

By age 9, Ledecky wrote bigger and bigger swimming goals in a notebook. And she was achieving all of them. Everyone knew she was going to be a swimming star.

>>> Ledecky's parents helping during one of her high school swim meet.

To be the best, you must work with the best. At age 10, Ledecky began training with coach Yuri Suguiyama. He was the first of many world-class coaches for Ledecky. He taught Ledecky how to be strong and fast in the water. He explained the importance of **tempo** and pacing.

"She is a fierce competitor who hates to lose and is mentally tough," Suguiyama said.

FACT

In 2006, Ledecky met Olympic swimming champion Michael Phelps and got his autograph. Six years later, she was on the Olympic team with him!

>>> Ledecky (top left) laughs with her Stone Ridge teammates before a competition in 2015.

From pre-K to high school, Ledecky attended Catholic schools. Her high school was Stone Ridge School of the Sacred Heart in Bethesda, Maryland.

Ledecky loved swimming, but she enjoyed other activities too. She took piano lessons and played basketball and soccer. But after breaking her arm in gym class in fourth grade, she gave up the other sports. Ledecky put all her focus into swimming.

〉〉〉 Ledecky celebrates her win during a junior
national swimming championship in 2011.

Ledecky took her potential seriously. Her dad
would drive her to the pool at 4:15 a.m. to train.
Her mom would pick her up at 7 a.m. with breakfast
and take her to school. She practiced after school
each day as well.

It soon became clear that the longer the race, the better she did. Other swimmers lost their focus or got tired after so many laps. Not Ledecky. She kept going like a machine.

>>> Ledecky swims in a high school championship in 2013, helping her team win.

During her sophomore year of high school, Ledecky achieved something truly amazing. She set a U.S. record in the 500-yard freestyle! At the same time, she trained harder than ever to qualify for the 2012 London Olympics.

Family Connections

Sports really do run in the Ledecky family. Katie's uncle Jon Ledecky is co-owner of the New York Islanders hockey team. Because he was involved in professional sports, Katie met a lot of famous athletes. There's even a video of basketball great Michael Jordan with her in an owner's box at a hockey game.

When Ledecky graduated high school, she held every school swimming record except one—the 100-yard breaststroke.

〉〉〉 Ledecky swims the breaststroke leg of the 200-yard medley event for her high school team as a senior.

CHAPTER TWO

THE OLYMPICS

In London, Ledecky stunned the world. She won the gold medal in the 800-meter freestyle by more than four seconds. However, her life didn't change much. When she returned to school, her classmates treated her the same. Ledecky appreciated things being normal again.

Despite her success, she kept working harder. Ledecky was USA Swimming's Athlete of the Year three years in a row. But she wanted to be the best. Ledecky chose to delay going to college to train for the 2016 Olympics.

FACT

Many of Ledecky's high school friends and teachers traveled to support her in the Olympics and other competitions.

>>> Ledecky couldn't stop smiling after winning her first Olympic gold medal.

>>> Ledecky focuses before an
Olympic race.

The 2016 Olympics were in Rio de Janeiro, Brazil.
Ledecky once again powered her way to victory. She
earned four gold medals and a silver.

Ledecky returned home to attend Stanford University
in California. She helped its swim team win back-to-back
NCAA championships. Along the way, she set 11 U.S.
and 15 NCAA records. She also received the Honda Cup,
given to the country's top female college athlete.

"I had a lot of fun and made some friends that I'll
have forever," Ledecky said.

But it was time for a change. After two years of college swimming, Ledecky turned pro. As a pro, she could have earned between $5 and $8 million or more in **endorsements** after the 2016 Olympics. But student athletes weren't allowed to be paid.

>>> Ledecky's five 2016 Olympic medals

FACT

As of June 2021, college athletes are allowed to make money off their names, images, and likenesses.

CHAPTER THREE
CHALLENGES

At the 2019 FINA World Championships in South Korea, Ledecky got sick. She had to pull out of two events. She still won a gold medal in the 800-meter freestyle. But the winning time wasn't her best. "I was incredibly disappointed," Ledecky said afterward.

However, she wasn't disappointed about her times or lack of medals. She was disappointed that she missed a chance to compete. That's all that ever really mattered to her.

And then came the worldwide **COVID-19 pandemic**. The 2020 Tokyo Olympics were postponed for a year. Ledecky took online classes to finish her psychology degree. She continued to train as well. However, she couldn't train with other people because of the pandemic. Instead, she trained in a 25-yard (23-meter) private pool.

〉〉〉 Despite feeling sick, Ledecky powered through her 800-meter freestyle heats.

>>> Ledecky swims to win an Olympic gold medal in the 800-meter freestyle event at the Tokyo Olympics in 2021.

When the delayed Olympics finally happened, Ledecky blasted ahead of the competition. She won two gold and two silver medals. She followed that up with four more gold medals at the 2022 World Aquatics Championships.

A few months later, she broke the world record for the 1,500-meter short course and the 800-meter freestyle in other competitions. Without a doubt, Ledecky was the GOAT (Greatest of All Time) of women's swimming.

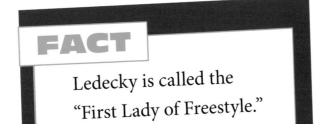

FACT

Ledecky is called the "First Lady of Freestyle."

CHAPTER FOUR
GIVING BACK

Ledecky is a swimming superstar. She's also a kind, giving person. She supports and encourages her teammates and opponents. Ledecky knows that everyone is working hard and doing their best.

Ledecky's kindness isn't limited to the pool. She helps others by partnering with multiple charities. She participates in USA Swimming Foundation's Golden Goggles Awards and the Wounded Warriors Project.

Another charity Ledecky supports is Swim Across America. This organization raises money for cancer research and patient programs.

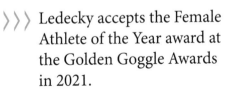

>>> Ledecky accepts the Female Athlete of the Year award at the Golden Goggle Awards in 2021.

At Stanford, Ledecky learned to love biking because she didn't have a driver's license. This love led her to partner with Bikes for the World. This organization makes used bikes available to low-income people in developing countries.

〉〉〉 Ledecky talks to reporters at a press conference in 2018.

Ledecky also enjoys visiting schools and giving motivational talks. She shares her experiences, talks about the challenges she's faced, and encourages students to follow their dreams. She teaches them about the importance of swimming and water safety too.

Got Milk?

Ledecky once swam a full pool length with a glass of chocolate milk on her head to promote the #gotmilkchallenge. Talk about impressive balance!

CHAPTER FIVE

THE FUTURE

Ledecky was once the youngest Olympian on Team USA. Now she's a swimming legend. She has won 10 Olympic medals and 21 world championships. She has also broken 16 world records.

In July 2023, Ledecky won her sixteenth individual world swimming title. This moved her past Michael Phelps for the most career individual titles. She also became the first swimmer to win six consecutive world championships in the same event—the 800-meter freestyle.

People admire her because she's humble and hardworking. "I'm lucky to have a family that loves me whether I swim really well or swim poorly, or don't swim at all," she says.

>>> Ledecky cheers after winning the
1,500-meter freestyle during the World
Aquatics Championships in July 2023.

Ledecky shows no signs of slowing down. She continues to train steadily, break records, and inspire people around the world. Next on her to-do list? **Dominate** the 2024 Paris Olympics.

"There's so much more to life than swimming and the Olympics," Ledecky admits, "and the people around me remind me of that." But until she moves on from swimming entirely, she'll be setting records and making waves.

TIMELINE

1997 Born on March 17 in Washington, D.C.

2003 Begins swimming for the Palisades Swim Team

2010 Qualifies for her first U.S. Summer National Meet

2012 Wins a gold medal in her first Olympics in London

2013 Breaks two world records at the World Aquatics Championships

2015 Sets three world records and wins five gold medals at the World Championships

2016 Wins five medals at the Rio Olympics

2016 Enrolls at Stanford University and joins their swim team

2017 Breaks her own world record in the 1500-meter freestyle and wins six medals at the World Championships

2019 Wins three medals at the World Aquatics Championships despite facing illness

2020 Graduates from Stanford University

2021 Wins four medals at the Tokyo Olympics

2022 Sets new world record in the 800-meter freestyle at the U.S. National Championships

2023 Surpasses Michael Phelps for the most career individual world swimming titles with 16

GLOSSARY

COVID-19 (KO-vid nine-TEEN)—a mild to severe respiratory illness that is caused by a coronavirus

DOMINATE (DAH-muh-nayt)—to be superior or excel in a particular field or activity

ENDORSEMENTS (in-DOR-smuhnts)—agreements where a company pays an athlete to promote their products

FREESTYLE (FREE-stile)—a style of swimming where the competitors choose their stroke, but most choose the front crawl as it's the fastest

HEAT (HEET)—a preliminary round in a swimming competition, where the fastest swimmers advance to the final races

PANDEMIC (pan-DEH-mik)—a disease that spreads over a wide area and affects many people

TEMPO (TEM-poh)—in swimming, the rhythm or speed at which a swimmer strokes

WAKE (WAYK)—the trail or series of ripples behind a swimmer

READ MORE

Fishman, Jon M. *Katie Ledecky*. Minneapolis: Lerner Publications, 2021.

Ignotofsky, Rachel. *Women in Sports: 50 Fearless Athletes Who Played to Win*. Berkeley, CA: Ten Speed Press, 2017.

Scheff, Matt. *Katie Ledecky*. Minneapolis: Abdo, 2017.

INTERNET SITES

Katie Ledecky
katieledeckyswim.com

Olympics: Swimming
olympics.com/en/sports/swimming

Team USA: Katie Ledecky
teamusa.com/profiles/katie-ledecky-851377

INDEX

AUTHOR BIO

Ryan G. Van Cleave is the author of dozens of books for children and hundreds of articles published in magazines. As The Picture Book Whisperer, they help celebrities write books for children. Ryan lives in Florida.